# city of ladies

*New Women's Voices Series, No. 152*

poems by

# et.stark

Finishing Line Press
Georgetown, Kentucky

# city of ladies

*New Women's Voices Series, No. 152*

*for my mother and grandmother,
two unapologetically-strong women*

Copyright © 2020 by et.stark
ISBN 978-1-64662-281-8 First Edition
All rights reserved under International and Pan-American Copyright Conventions. No part of this book may be reproduced in any manner whatsoever without written permission from the publisher, except in the case of brief quotations embodied in critical articles and reviews.

Publisher: Leah Maines

Editor: Christen Kincaid

Cover Art: et.stark

Author Photo: Alexandra Tjoelker

Cover Design: Elizabeth Maines McCleavy

Order online: www.finishinglinepress.com
also available on amazon.com

Author inquiries and mail orders:
Finishing Line Press
P. O. Box 1626
Georgetown, Kentucky 40324
U. S. A.

# Table of Contents

A Good Wife's Guide ............................................................. 1

grin and bare-it ..................................................................... 4

My mother left me at the zoo ............................................. 5

Lie Back (itwillbeoversoon) ................................................ 8

Do you feel safe? ................................................................ 11

Paradiso ............................................................................... 14

plant your flag .................................................................... 17

*Behave Like a Beauty* ......................................................... *19*

ecological disturbance ...................................................... 21

Danaus plexippus .............................................................. 23

[A WOMAN WALKS INTO A BAR] ............................... 25

city of ladies ....................................................................... 27

*Stalking the Girl* ................................................................. *29*

most-likely conclusion ..................................................... 31

Reveal, in motion .............................................................. 33

## A Good Wife's Guide

I. ~~Have dinner ready~~ Is it strange that I prefer
the skin on cooling milk? Certain words are
edible, like rose-cream and nasturtium.
Let's return to a time where all the mattresses
are standard-sized and I slept with my knees folded
under hip.

II. Speak softly. I borrowed bluer words for my toast.
It's my favorite flavor. People tell me it is
only a color and I think, that is why no one will
taste you. You don't even know how to use your
eyes.

III. Remember when we used to sit in mushroom rings
trying to feed the fairies unsalted peanut butter and raisins?
I carried a luckier-horseshoe. But it fell through
the horseshoe shaped hole in my pocket.

IV. Some animals kiss out of jealousy. Out of
ownership. Or we can't explain it at all.

V. ~~Clear away the clutter~~ Sometimes I knock
the ember into the ashtray, to watch it smoke
outside my dense lungs. Winter came right-on-schedule
this year. Thankfully, I can still see
my own shadow.

VI. There are only a certain number of
shipwreck-excuses for living underwater.

VII. Sometimes I do paint pictures.

VIII. We went to school together, sat on
the same swing. No. I have never broken any bones.
What a strange way to ask for one of my hands.

IX. ~~Be happy~~ I bled from my wrist onto a sliced
persimmon. Or I sliced my wrist with a full-blooded
persimmon. I wonder if my unripe skin would also
numb your tongue. You can lift me off the page
using only your spit and a patch
of bare flesh.

X. Poison oak is not only skin-toxic. But look
how my coat shines under the imitation sun.
I've combed my finest hairs. Repeatedly rinsed
my soiled selves.

XI. You taught me how to speak but I lost
the perpendicular-sounds. So I read a book
on taxidermy and filled my mouth with sand.
It is best to stitch with sinew. The challenge is
the eyes, and the putting everything back together.

XII. ~~Greet him~~ High up or higher spoken,
the g(-)ds chirp like famished rodents, fighting
over moldy suet and pre-nuptials. Feed the birds,
certainly. Maybe also a stray-something. Never
feed yourself from your own planted garden.

XIII. They should stop naming streets after people.
I'm tired of stepping over crumpled bones
and running into old friends. We could move
where dirt is iron-bound and the men wear patches
to show where they have been. There is
still a part of me that remains
uninhabited.

XIV. ~~Arrange his pillow~~ Because recently
I've been spending time on singular thoughts.
How many analogies use falling fruit?
I know of at least two.

XV. A word is suddenly whole upon departure.
I've never taken someone's head. I've worked
the binding and sealed the edges with a match.
Ask your lonely daughter.

XVI. Try flapping your arms. No,
it doesn't look strange. Each wing
is individually feathered.
For the ritual after-dinner.

XVII. ~~A good wife always~~ Remember,
it is exactly what you've wanted.
For years.

*Italicized excerpts taken from "The good wife's guide", author unknown, *Housekeeping Monthly*, May 13, 1955

**grin and bare-it**

(nicht)/nicht-schwanger/:

(my daughter)/i used to love long train rides. [1]


(intimate)/immediate/:

(a queen bee)/i will emerge fully formed in a matter of 14-16 days.[2]


(pre-)/post-/:

(——) being the operative word.[3]


[1] the first (practical)/steam locomotive was built in (1804)/1812. The first train related accident occurred in (1830)/1832. (39)/37 years later, the transcontinental railroad was completed.

[2] the (average)/worker bee requires (21)/22 days to hatch, despite her smaller size.

[3] sometimes (you)/i fall asleep with an analog clock against (my)/our ear.

## My mother left me at the zoo

On the second day, I still believed her.
It wasn't how I imagined it would be,
with trees and little moats.
To my surprise, it was only a theatre lined in velvet.

I met the zookeeper.

A scarlet tanager told me
                not to smile, that it's not what they pay for.

What do they pay for?
She said

I was in the next act, and I'd better hurry, because the lion
was almost finished eating the painted gazelle.

On the fifth day, I made opening act.
I pretend I am at a ball and I know
how to waltz. Know
how to sever all my toes and walk the red-carpet.

While I am head-dancing my body
removes one button at a time.
Occasionally, the audience is many,
on bad-days, rain-days,
                one.

I only ever saw the birds.
Speaking tongues, singing silent-riddles.
I rebuild the night sky
from all I remember in a book on celestial navigation.

Are all the stars animal-shaped? Or
am I once again mistaking mirrors for constellations.

It can be lonely at the zoo,
and there aren't nearly as many
balloons as I had hoped.

If I could choose my life I would never
sleep indoors. Lay myself along the tundra
and wait for purple-blossoms to climb
my throat, root in my garden-dense lungs.

I want to be furthest-North.
Want to be alone when I touch
my own skin.

I wish I knew how to grow fur.
How to crawl on all fours and snarl
with my carnivore-mouth.

Wish I could see in the dark or
land on all of my feet.

Yesterday, the zookeeper told me
I was looking worn out. I said,
I am still a little girl
making wreathes out of daisies, and I swear
I didn't smile.

Onstage I bend forward
and hold my own ankles like a manacle.
Can rest on my knees and touch my forehead
to the wet-floor in prayer.

The elephants were sent back to Africa
without their ivory teeth.
Will I go home too? I have already lost a tooth
and something else entirely.

Tonight I will stun the crowd.
I am mercurial and a hydrogen star.
Collecting roses between
my legs instead of at my feet.
A brilliant display of dead-light.

Bravo, they will say,
Once more.

On the first day, my mother said,
wait here.
By the gift shop, next to the broken fountain.
She said,
I'll be right back.

## Lie Back  (itwillbeoversoon)

i.
I've forgotten to write down
the genus and species of sheep that have

seen a wolf. Surrendered to the cliché
of losing things in the shortest-terms.

How did I spend an hour watching
an ibex climb up and down a mountain,

in hi-def
and still not know what it means to hunt.

I say myself hunter
then hunted-into not hunted for.

The relationship between lamb's blood and the soil
is another way to say intimate and then

take it back very-quickly. Vulture wings look
like hands from here, so I wave.


ii.
I asked to sip from
your menstrual cup because I

have never been to church. Never found a
union worth crossing-myself for. It isn't

so savage to want to taste The Body
and-then-some. People keep inviting me

to eat them and then getting upset when
I bring a fork. So tender that

its bones fell off. So tender
that it fell into-bone.

I studied arithmetic by pulling
out my baby teeth. I found

them in my mother's dressing-drawer and said
these couldn't-possibly-be mine.


iii.
I've spent a long time imagining
Dorothy walking into technicolor.

Am not-so-brave that a lunar pull won't affect my tide. Or
is it the other way around? In fact I've

been confusing causation with a wet envelope
that reads: tear these edges off first, which

I picked up along with a trophy someone else
won the year I was born. Apigee is the way

I chart my nearness to people who can
know what I have or have-not-done. Or

how many planes and trains run through my-night.
It's all political really, being born, I tell a doped-up

Judy Garland. We swallow another pill and she shrugs,
I only wanted my g(-)ddamned dog.


iv.
The left side of my abdomen
still reads: student driver and it

is checkered across my pelvic bone.
I am filling measureable-space with me

and my, which used to say particular-acceleration.
I promise it isn't always about the dangerous tone

of a wasp-filled bird. Telling me to
stopstopstop putting paper masks of

people-i-knew
on every fractured canine skull I find in the road.

But I can't help myself if everyone-keeps-smiling
and I just want-to-want to see the parade.

Some arthropods are marked by cellular memories and I am
afraid that I am not.


v.
I said I would yes
because yes I am a notary public

and there is a transparent film
between my dermal layers.

It's a filter for a pressurized tank
to store all the soft-bodied squid
I scooped off the ocean floor.

Did you plan a menu before
we slid the knife into the spineless-spine-and

before we trimmed the stem off a growing-thing?
Sacrifice is only sacrificial if

you do it in-my-name.
Barely there and still I bless you 2x2.

Sacrifice is only
                yesyesyesyesyes.

**Do you feel safe?**

I say the branches of a tree grow in the direction
of the wind or-the-sun or indiscriminately or
maybe that's sunflowers.

I wish I grew seeds for the sparrows to eat.
The wind moves in a direction-opposite
to holy-grain. Have swallowed

painted bricks that crumbled and lifted
brambles over cities-of-Men
and women who wrote songs

about women-loving-women.

The cold-truth is I don't recall whether
we grew feathers or fur or hooves first.
Foremost there is wine for dulling our sensibilities,

there is dried corn for filling our burlap bodies
and telling crows to come forth and feast
on gathering-bodies.

My flesh is smoked adipose and
wrangled into the best galleries of female
forms which cater to absolved-carrion.

Eventually they hung us all,
on fallen-down rafters nailed together
into t-shapes that relinquished our sins.

So that our fathers could sleep quiet knowing
we were halted, in our
prepped-and-primed. The harbingers of ending

said not-now. And we rose again.

How many does it take to wrangle
a herd of blasphemous, cleft-footed disciples.
But these spiny tails spell damned

and darned for the coming-season.
Welcome the holy-days which pine
then cull for our past transgressions.

Women decided the future.
Decided to crucify the sooth-sayers
who said we were tempting-the-tempters.

Coddle your first-born.
Cradle your birthed-sons and
tell them this is who you're meant to be.

An elliptical orbit anticipates the obstacles
which inhibit the expected value,
which is pursuant to an oral-code for taking.

Mythologically speaking the labyrinth is not
guarded at both ends. The way
an ionic union borrows positive traits

to bury the negative union of one
g(-)d to another.
Heretical whores call it divine, then

put a saddle on the finest linens
and claim that cotton has no memory of
cold-woven lineage.

There is another term for supple cantors.

Then
ambition calls itself the rightful heir
for peasants and females who serve

the old-g(-)ds.
Demand the sacrifice of virgins who've run out
of streaming services.

So we resurrect a firewall.
And I pray-and-pray for the messiah
to tell us it has eclipsed the end.

The triad of past-present-now
has forgotten how to sew.
I have forgotten how to stitch-simple.

Good-guys win, they keep telling us.
And bad-women lose the thread.
The failure of most cosmological theorems is straw.

We are unfit for a rapture built by raptors.

I lost my needle in a stack
of other lost-needles.
Of many, many other needles.

## Paradiso

Tell me your darkest fantasy and
I will tell you how I cry looking at
blue herons on a river.

Touch yourself and point out
the place where Sisyphus gave
up.

Let it all roll backwards

So I lost my tour guide to the asphodels
in my hair.
I thought they were pretty and

you said
poison poison-poisonous,
for two.

Or twelve or there are arachnids whose
legs twitch when the terms of war are
brought to light.

I want to go inside only I am
already rooted to the sofa, pulling dust
notes from under my tongue and

testing air quality to retrieve a
perfect sample of polluted breath that
fills the atmosphere and melted

the glacier preserving g(-)d
and the wooly mammoth.

In the Cretaceous era I swig whiskey at
the saloon next to a layer of snake skin

that someone said I sloughed off, so
would I mind, really-mind

picking up after myself and shouting
last-calls into the mouth of something
quite-divine.

I wrapped clothesline around your wrists
and strung you up to dry in the white sun
because I am a domestic bird.

Preening my tail feathers and ingesting a virus that
shrivels my flight-muscles

Black and white feathers on the still-water
mark the place where I swam down and
Away.

If there are twenty four vibrating strings between
us how are there not twenty five?

I can't stop repeating the traveler's prayer
for good luck and safer-passage and the electrical equivalent
of purchasing too much propane for me to swallow.

I spent all my eyelashes hoping
to be contained by the orbit of a charged particle.

Someone once described an atom as plum pudding
so it makes sense that I want to run
a fork into your stomach and pluck

your electrons to wear on my fingertips like
black olives.

Perform the piece in whole.
Wholly perform the piece.
It is holy you are holy
I am

divine in the sense of unbaptised pagans and women
who wear practical shoes.

Condemn my violent inclinations to cull myself while
you're inside me and shove a wafer against my tongue between
your hardened nipple and my

wolf-teeth.
The ones that founded Rome and found a place in
your skin to build a greater-cityscape.

I deserve
a slap on the wrist, across my face, against,
your bruised knuckle or a ruler that has measured

the distance from one savior to another.
It should be a thousand years but sometimes

it skips a few the way I skipped school
and practiced blood-letting
instead.

I fell asleep in a public park and woke
with another head in my lap.
With my fingers tangled in mud streaked hair.

I said
are you a g(-)d?
At the same time it said
please,
do you know any other songs?

**plant your flag**

i said free the nipple
but the truth is i feel-safest in
my cage with them still attached
or

better-yet
between your unwashed teeth

and for that matter i'd like to fit
all-my-skin against the grooves in
the dome of your mouth

why does the fungus on a dead log know
how to smile prettier-than
i do

if-i-grow-up
i want to be an insect that hatched underground

or a tulip bulb that
i might sprout beautiful and unscented

i wish i was
in a line of furred-things
following a larger furred-thing
in search of being hungry

asked a gray goose to tell me where
it keeps its gold
asked a gray-man if he would consider
letting me pass un-loved

because on warm days i am a little thing playing
hardest-to-get

i told a brown recluse she was stunning
at the same time a stranger placed his
index finger on the back of my knee

and declared:
i bet no one has touched you like-this
before

## Behave Like a Beauty

*A beauty behaves kindly, confidently, beautifully.*
(Sometimes I feel like I have slaughtered all the lambs.
Or I am old-western wielding two guns,
my legs around a saddle. I've broken my own rule.)

*You can walk like a beauty.*
(I swore I adored you, and I do.
I adore the way my skin rises to blister on the heat.
I sipped antifreeze cocktails on the porch,
when it was summer and we were rabbits hunting.
Only a hare is born furred, with its eyes wide open.)

*Keep your back straight. Teach your hips to move forward.*
(I know what I deserve.)

*Like a beauty, you can keep a serene face.*
(Admire me, for a time.
I have always been a prisoner. I have always been
this wet-prison and so many territories to be conquered.
I gutted my mother, stopped using my child-shaped mouth.)

*A beauty doesn't bid for attention.*
(Once I made a finger painting of Virgin Mary
but she didn't turn out, called it Firework and signed my name.
Did you tell me that my eyes were beautiful?
They are blue and sea-red and I said thank you,
even though you couldn't see them. Is this really all
that I am good for?)

*How often do you really need to raise your eyebrows?*
(Here is what I know:
A desert-wasp set her eggs gently under my tongue,
for safekeeping. Occasionally my lover is a fish,
abandoning our children in tall-grasses. Some of these boys
have us outnumbered. Would it make a difference
if I asked nicely?)

*You can dress like a beauty.*
(My father is a narcissist and ate us one after another.
I can no longer count to ten with my mother's native-tongue.
It is possible I used to be someone else.
You ruined my last eggshell dinner gown. But I invited you in,
so it's ok, right?)

*You can be groomed like a beauty, stockings smooth and straight.*
(I'm sorry.
My throat has calcified and I swallowed
most of the colored stones. Did I answer
the Important question?)

*A beauty doesn't rely on variety.*
(Yes, I have been looking forward
to this all my wholesome-life.)

*You have to remember, if you want to be a beauty, no vandalism.*
(Of course I am happy.
I have never been so happy.)

\* Italicized excerpts taken from: 'Not every woman can be a beauty but every woman can behave like a Beauty' by Mrs. Walter Denigre Sohier, who was Wendy Burden before her recent marriage, *Vogue*, February 1950

**ecological disturbance**

every significant moment in my life
has been marred by the flight-of birds
in the wrong hour

who first decided it was okay to eat
fish
who decided it was
only-fish

my spine can be extracted in a single motion

i came
pre-cleaned and then dirtied
on-the-knife

gulped down all the wishful coins
because i am jealous of your legs
keep my hidden-teeth until you feel safe

enough to dip your toes

someone tried to warn me that the lake
was toxic
i grin tooth-first and flex my gills

how do you think it got that way

i perform a lazy-breast stroke
and blow thought-out bubbles into the
lungs of a tadpole

my savior is still waving
from the shore and making the sign for
poison with his hand against a throat

i mirror his gesture
as my crown-of kelp dries mud
crawling with sunfish eggs into
opened eyes

and i wave back

## Danaus plexippus

I have been hunting the hunted thing for every meal. Hungry,
hungry like a hurt-thing that has been soaking
and drinking river-water in place of
soil-stained tissue. I also kill more than a crocodile
preparing to rattle into spheres. Like water
like washed-out ships drowning in clay pots. You
grow succulents. Grow succulents because you like it dry
and
I am thirsty for the theory-of a fish that is
my mother.
Loving other-mothers who loved what might-have-been me
and father says it is a bear,
around or through and under-over the stream in a forest that
chased us all-the-way home.

I said dance on my grave, we danced on
my grave. Our-graves were selected with all-the-love our parents
possessed. And I dance a dance that
dances for a place in-the-line. I read once that there is a time
when things are thin
and molecules vibrate and we can see
the dead on certain-days and I hope
and hope that is
not-true. Up high, I am nervous every time I see the area code
of where I was born. Because I know we said always
but
I'm tired of unmarked-numbers telling me
who is dead now.

We carry it forward. Now we say I-am-
sorry for miscommunications on the orbit of certain handmade-
things. Physicists
invented a new form of light based on a theory about caterpillars
who scream in fear. I scream to prepare myself for how other people
scream in fear. So
I studied the life cycle of growing-wings.

Some say king-
or-queen of flying to decapitated-forests and around
the flattened mountains. So I said goodbye and got all
wet-around the eyes, because I can't see
how you can apologize but then
am not sure if I mean it.

I flew home. I flew-into and
underneath a thermal sediment that is resistant
to the new-enlightenment. Newly-lit
and lightly feathered is the only way to fall
screaming from the sky.

I have been hunting-hunter-hunted and all I want to draw is wolves
and teeth and a dried umbilical cord against
a bluish-neck. And the wax.

I used to raise them,
you know.
In a screen inside the lining of my gut. We rode
bicycles, and picked them up and
they screamed
and

I didn't hear it.

## [A WOMAN WALKS INTO A BAR]

Man: Can I buy you a drink?

Woman: Thank you, I have one.

M: You have the most beautiful eyes.

## [A WOMAN LOOKS AWAY]

M: you have the most beautiful
here is a list of-why
you should be a little closer to
my greased-up tongue I want
you to feel safer-than you ever
have a drink by the
water is rushing against my ear
drums you don't know by-heart what
you're missing your
mother said it was OK
you
might be my mother if only
you were born in the same month i lost
my innocence is cute-on-you and
i heard you wanted to be heard so
i will nod-and-nod while i strip away
your maiden's-name is
mine

W: I am waiting—

M: for someone to prove
you are just a tiny-squirrel looking for
a safe-place to build your nest in
a tall-tall tree and
i will barter my lofty branches for
your simple-smile which saves
the words for yes-and-no in the most delicious way

W: I am—

M: save your breath for when i rob you
of-it
everyone knows you are waiting for
a mad-boy to make you good-good
good

W: I—

M: don't strain those pretty lips for
all the loss in babylon for
a paradise without bearing-fruit
and
i can get quite-angry

[A WOMAN CLOSES HER EYES]

M: you don't have to tell me
how warm you are

**city of ladies**

it's not that i don't-want-it
but that i forget how to smirk around
a dinner fork

said i was a doctor and sliced
away a square of your innermost-thigh

let the root vegetables sweat-it-out
together
the key is to sear each side on
a high heat

carbon-ash on my tongue and you
are all but over-done
i can wear a suit to meet your parents
but can't promise not to take my meals

on-the-floor
like i was taught
like a-good-girl

better girls learn to make flowered-bracelets
and coo at babies
and march-march-
march to the beat of some

days are cut from the same linen i used
to bind my feet into: a cocoon
of pretty-bones
into:
a dreamcatcher

they told us we would come-out-of-this
winged
come-out of this
whole

i can't stop laughing over the consonants
in consent

wore a shirt that read:
badboy
and an elderly lady told her husband to:
let the nice young man go first

i
can't stop-grinning
hollow out your candlesticks in case they
come-back

i'd be a nun if only i could
keep my g(-)d-damned knees together

this summer i became an antarctic fish
i know this because they found antifreeze
in my stomach
in my veins

abstinence is the cure to every compulsion
when i was twelve they gave me a pen that wrote
just-say-no

so why is it:
i-can't

## Stalking the Girl

Where do we go from here
is such a stupid question.

There is no vector without direction. I know
what I promised. But I thought you knew how to
ingest whole lies like swords.

And if I did it for my g(-)d
why am I the only one at my first baptism? I went
for a swim anyway. Held my own head down.

How is every mass about cannibalism?
I've consumed so many bodies already. He must
have been freeze-dried and sliced evenly.

This is what the astronauts ate. Way up
in metal bowls. Trading crisp-body for
blood like Tang.

23 meters below. Near the mountain peaks
there is land for sale. Promising unseen
views and little oxygen.

Dense water depends on polar ice. I also
depend on a simple vanishing act. Catching
small brown moths to practice mimicry.

Why do I buy so many tea lights and invitations
to parties I will never host? I think I am fond
of the open ocean because I am terrified.

Remind me why my hands are no longer webbed.
I have never been the strongest-swimmer. But
I can tread for days.

Drinking gin to remember my aquatic life.
Who ever thought they could make a candle
smell like sun-dried laundry?

It was supposed to be a gorgeous rendition
of a famous opera. But we left our sheet music,
left where we were.

Some of us showed up the next day.

The trick is
to say thank you
to show sincerity in your desire to

please
you have no right to questions.
*It's a lot like getting paid to sample fine wine.*

\*italicized excerpts taken from 'Stalking the Girl"
*Girl Watcher Magazine*, pg 14, June 1959

## most-likely conclusion

i love how standing water smells
like dead-things even when it
is completely empty

do you blame me
for-it-all
because you-should

i excel at topography
and not showing up in the coordinates
i promise

you told me to stop-saying
so i will say i think it
is unfair when people bring more
than twelve items to the express lane

it's too late
for all-of-that

i hate abstraction but
will claim that dragonflies make me
nervous because they hunt the queen

g(-)d-rest
the many of us who falter
between sips or
eat too many seed to break the fast

i've lost-it
that thing they said i had
or more accurately

i traded-it
for an angry bouquet of paradise-birds

i threaded the skull
of a rodent on a piece of wet leather
and called it
enough

**Reveal, in motion**


Imagine that the solution to your life
was written on a plastic board
and bolted to a telephone pole.

So everything depended on turning
the right corner or crossing the street
without looking in any direction.

It is tacked below a sign offering
cash for unused diabetic test strips.
Above someone who wants to buy your
uninhabitable home.

So that instead of spending months
unfolding protons into several dimensions
you could read your intentions
in permanent marker and ALL CAPS.

I wanted to be glorious too.

We might have avoided all this trouble
by crushing small hive beetles under gloved thumbs
and relishing the cracking exoskeleton without remorse.

Don't rough yourself up for missing the boat
that launched on time.
For reading the wrong-sign and not knowing
what moon you were born under.

We all learn to confuse water for wine
and immediacy for intimacy.
There is a handwritten oil to egg ratio
taped to a cabinet door.

Lift up the last remaining card on the table.
Press it to your forehead and concentrate.
Really concentrate.

About the last time I saw you,
is this
      your card?

**et.stark** is a Michigan-born poet, bee-lover, and artist. She was the Book Arts Fellow at Press 43, in association with the Chapbook/Broadside Collaborative and ExpressNewark while attending Rutgers University MFA for creative writing. Most recently she published i (don't) have a spare tire on my car, a chapbook with Kattywompus Press and some of her poems can be found in *Prelude*.

www.ingramcontent.com/pod-product-compliance
Lightning Source LLC
LaVergne TN
LVHW040117080426
835507LV00041B/1342